The Ghetto Effect and the Urban Traumatic Stress Syndrome (UTSS)

KEITH HICKMAN

authorHOUSE®

AuthorHouse™
1663 Liberty Drive
Bloomington, IN 47403
www.authorhouse.com
Phone: 1 (800) 839-8640

Published by AuthorHouse   07/09/2015

ISBN: 978-1-5049-1732-2 (sc)
ISBN: 978-1-5049-1731-5 (e)

Print information available on the last page.

This book is printed on acid-free paper.

Scripture quotations marked NIV are taken from the Holy Bible, New International Version®. NIV®. Copyright © 1973, 1978, 1984 by International Bible Society. Used by permission of Zondervan. All rights reserved. [Biblica]

Contents

{WARNING CONTENTS MAY CAUSE EMOTIONAL DRAMA}

This book is not based upon scientific research and study. Nor is it based upon someone who has spent his or her life in academia. I am just your average American Joe who has been blessed to see every aspect of American society first hand. This book is not intended to appease anyone. If it causes you to find hate in your heart or want to run out and change things. Then this is good, for you should feel something when reading its contents. The root cause of the Ghetto Effect is government, which dictates the very essence of it with industrial will. It is in effect the very essence of what ills America today. It's the thing that no one wants to admit is causing harm through moral and ethical decay. The ghetto is no longer based on the color of ones skin, but economics and percentage of criminals in a specific area. Since the year 2000, when the Mayor of New York decided to get tough on crime, and all other major cities followed. His heart was in the right place, but it left out the humanistic side of society. The police are no longer serving and protecting the citizens, but practicing professional law enforcement. When an area has say over 60% of its citizens are criminals. Then the police have the right to do whatever they have to, in order to enforce the law. The politicians see this as a great thing, because of the statistics in crime reduction. The citizens in the suburbs are seeing on the news how effective this approach is. The politicians are getting elected over this, and the poor, ill educated and dissolute of society takes the blunt of it. So born out of the ignorance of our society the Ghetto Effect emerges.

CHAPTER 1

The Logic Behind the Name

I had originally wanted to write a book on my philosophy of ISM's and Conundrums. Instead this serendipitous idea arose instead. It is an idea that has caused me to have emotion and behavior problems in academia and life. It is an inescapable realism that I have had to face. The logic behind the idea is very simplistic. It starts with the beginning of mankind, and then goes to God likeness in morality, ethnics, and government. It is hundred and eighty degrees out of phase with American values and beliefs. But this Ghetto Effect has infected our society like the plague. It has altered history from a path of goodness to a path of un-righteousness. It has been slowly eroding the social structure of peoples lives without them even noticing. It is the same thing that we did to the American Indian.

All the politicians and school officials are looking to the experts in how to solve the problems with today's society. The problem is too broadly based to point to just one problem and throw money at it. In order to understand what the Ghetto Effect is. We must first break down the essence of it first.

If we look into history of mankind they were tribal at first, then warlords and finally Kings. In the New International Version of the Bible Genesis Chapter 6, Paragraph 1; "When men began to increase in number on the earth and daughters were born to them, 2 the sons of God saw the daughters of men were beautiful, and they married any they chose." Genesis Chapter 6, Paragraph 4; "…when the sons of God went to the daughters of men and had children by them. They were the heroes of old, men renown." The King James Version supports this: Genesis Chapter 6, Paragraph. 1; "AND it came to pass, when men began to multiply on the face of the earth, and daughters were born unto them, 2; That the sons of God saw the daughters of men were fair; and they took them wives of all which they chose." Genesis Chapter 6, Paragraph 4; "There were giants in the earth in those days: and also after that, when the sons of God came into the daughters of men, and they bare children to them, the same became mighty men which were of old, men of renown."

With this said it sounds like a contradictory of terms. For creationist and evolutionist would have us believe two different realities of existence. For there is a thing called microevolution and macroevolution. Where microevolution is where animals evolve out of their habitats. Vice macroevolution is more towards Darwinism, which has been proved wrong by DNA science. DNA shows us that this concept in proven wrong by the fact that human and ape DNA differ. There are similarities just as birds and other animals do. Just because a crow and an eagle have similar traits does not make them the same. For if man and ape were related there would have being born monkey-men by now. This does not mean one could not be a surrogate parent for the other. Even the Big Bang theory has merit where God spoke and life began. To think that everything was created out of chaos is like making a car out of junkyard with a tornado. We can see how God may have created man many times before through anthropology. But in the bible was the first time man was created in God image. So you can see how there is only three thousand years of God like men on the earth, and other men who are not. This division of science and religion has placed men in wars and division among themselves through pseudo-science. I feel that all things are possible. There is no doubting science because of the known properties of scientific laws that we know of. Because of these laws of the universe one would have to conceive that there would have to be some form of intelligent life that created everything. Not some tornado in space that just happened to make our world so perfectly balanced. Our universe may not be expanding, but instead traveling through space. The shifts in our magnetic fields could be our universe coming in close contact with other universes. This would cause ripple effects in our gravitational fields and thus cause string theory. With this said all things are possible. Only things that are good and are of truth come from God. These truths are self-evident that all men are created equal.

Then we have the Elitists, Socialists, Liberals, and Conservatives groups. The Elitists are the chosen few who were born out of poverty and are well educated. All of their basic needs are meet and money is not important to them. Because everything they have ever wanted they have had. Yet they feel though education that they are better than everyone else. They see employees and the poor as like children that need to be punished if they misbehave. They make themselves feel better by giving to charities, and supporting global warming, and recycling. Yet at the same time, they go to college with everything paid by the parents. They can come to class and sleep and still get a "C". They are the one's who go on all expense paid drunken vacations during spring break. As soon as they graduate they throw away all their hippy clothes, put on suites, and join corporate America.

The Socialist believes in the European design, and believes America should follow instead of lead the world. They are the sheep of society who cause a lot of discord between factions in both the democratic and the republican parties. Their agenda is anti American and most see them more as an annoyance than a threat.

Liberal America is the one's who are always fighting the good fight for the little guy, and the environment. The problem is they were programmed to respond only a few ways through Condition Reponses. These Reponses were developed in the school system using the means system, and television. Ask any liberal what they think, and the Reponses are always the same three answers. No they have no real ideas of their own. They have recently incorporated yelling instead of discussion, and rudely talking over others than waiting their turn. This and there is nothing a person does wrong, but only makes bad decisions. They believe in Situational Problems, instead of the person taking responsibility for their own action. Example: A young person goes into a store to buy something. They reach over and take money out of the register and leaves. They did not steal and it's not their fault, but the situation, and they were born poor. I would call this "Smothering," it's a combination of "mothering" and "smothering". This is where the "Nanny laws" are coming from. (Nanny Laws: are laws designed to over protect certain people with special rights. Instead of all laws being made for all the people without bias or reservations.) Liberals are always giving government more control over the people through programs that appear to help the poor. In reality they are giving more control to the few in government, and less rights to the people. They exchange the word right, to the word privilege. They also want to stand on the podium and yell about people rights. This is the same as why a liberal and a hard working employee make's a bad boss. The liberal is always trying to get out of work by bringing up others faults to the boss, so they can get away without doing anything. They are always on the bandwagon about how screwed up things are. If they were in charge, how things would be different. When they get in charge they will say "I know how screwed up things were, but I'm going to make things better. So I know how you have gotten out of work before, but now you have to tow the line." They are bound and determine to make sure you do more than what you did before. Which makes them a horrible boss. The hard worker never misses a day of work. They feel they know everything, and are the hardest working person there. In reality they are an average or below average worker. Since they are there all the time they don't feel they need to try very hard. They are never rested, and come in sick. Their attitude is callous, because they never take a vacation, and have fun. So when they get in charge they are out to make sure everyone is as miserable as they are.

Conservative Groups are the under valued and lest appreciated. This is because it does little to control the masses, but is great for financial gains. Conservative groups are always trying to decrease laws and regulations upon the people by the government. They are the hard working classes of people who want things to stay the way they have always been. They believe in God, Country and the American way. The Conservatives are not bad people nor is the Liberals. They both have the best interest of America in their hearts. What they have is two different agendas that are similar, but oppose each other. From all of this the Ghetto Effect is born.

CHAPTER 2

Manors, Morals, and Scruples

The idea of Kings came from men acting in a God like manner. For the word Goodness comes from the word Godly. The knights formed manners and scruples of old. Kings of old were placed in command of nations by Gods will. The Pope commanded the armies of England, France, and Spain at one time. Even the United States Constitution was conceived with Gods principles in mind, "In God We Trust". Things that are from God are undeniable truths that are self-evident to everyone who sees them. For all men were created equal in the sight of God, but in men's eyes they are not. This disparity is where the Ghetto Effect comes into play. For since the beginning of man he has tried to place himself above others and tried to achieve God-like status. Go to any big building and you find designated parking. This inequality is rampant throughout the world. This is why there will always be war. Because someone will always use the power given to him or her to depress another to raise he or she up.

Manors and Scruples pay an important part of our society. It has taken thousands of years to perfect them. Since the 1960's they have been under attack. This is a very serious dilemma to have. For without manners, morals, and scruples civilization is destined for destruction. Look at the classroom today vice yesterday. Yesterday the teacher ruled with an iron fist and a long stick. They took the chaos from the outside world and gave it order. The children were taught how to act appropriately and to think for themselves. Today there is chaos and disorder. The children are allowed to do whatever they want. In society people are not held responsible for there action, but rewarded for bad behavior. So, exactly how important is Manors, Morals and Scruples? Without manors there is no respect. How can a person respect the police, if the police do not respect the person? Without Morals there is no self-control. How can a child who has no control over themselves, prevent themselves from getting pregnant? Without Scruples there is no proper judgment. If a person is never taught self-respect, then how is that person going to respect others? In order to raise children you have love, respect and a structured environment, which gives them a sense of security. This is done by setting boundaries, establishing and enforcing rules. This disparity by only establishing rules of law and imprisonment to those who do not even understand why, is a lack of control. This is what we are doing to those people who we are imprisoning. It is all crime and punishment without love and respect. Without the love and respect that goes with the establishment of boundaries. The people are set to an endless game of cops and robbers. You show love and respect by having the people being apart of the healing process. Respect is having them set boundaries, and then being held accountable to it. Instead of disrespecting people by pulling guns on them, throwing them to the ground, and putting them in cages like animals. Talk to them with respect and a claim demeanor.

These things would not be put up with in middle class America. The citizens would have had the police fired, and the governor on the phone. Why because they are citizens and have the means, and know how to make change. Middle class America are law biding, gun carrying; do not mess with type of people. We say stop bulling in our schools, but not in our neighborhoods? This is because we have loss respect for them, and ourselves. As long as our moral and ethical behavior goes unchecked, this will still be a problem.

CHAPTER 3

Ghettos in America

The ghettos in America are a microism of this depression upon others. The first ghettos were from immigrants coming to this country. They had to work very hard to overcome the injustices and prejudices that held them down. They eventually lost their heritage, and assembled into the American way of life. They were able to do this, because they were all of European descent. Back when this country was starting out minorities and whites cohabitated. The Cherokee adapted to growing crops, and living side by side with the Europeans. There were white slaves as well as all others. Look at the Creoles of Southern Louisiana who were Spanish, French, and African decent. "(Webster's Ninth New Collegiate Dictionary: Creole: {...*crioulo* white person born in the colonies.} (1604) 1: a person of European descent born esp. in the West Indies or Spanish America 2: a white person descended from early French or Spanish settlers of the U.S. Gulf states and preserving their speech and culture 3: a person of mixed French or Spanish and Negro decent speaking a dialect spoken by many Negroes in southern Louisiana b: HAITTIAN c: *not cap:* a language based on two or more languages that serves as a native language of its speakers)." Please excuse the language of the old for the word that is defensive today was from the Spanish word meaning black. "Webster's Family Spanish-English Dictionary: black3 n 1: negro (color, raza) 2: negro m, -gra *f* (persona)".

The Great Awakenings in America, awoken the common American people to the word of God. Over half the population came to these revivals. "Wikipedia: Four great awakenings; 1st 1730's to 1743, 2nd 1800 to 1840, 3rd 1850's to 1900, and 4th 1960's to 1970's." Before the Great Awakenings Europe had its own which carried over to America. The bible was translated from Hebrew and Greek to English. England went from a Catholic religion to a Protestant religion. The first Great Awakening was a direct influence to the American Revolution. This transgression changed the mind set in all the cultures except America. America had their wealth in cotton, grain, and sugar products. This means manual labor and slavery was the only way to harvest the crops. Until the industrial revolution came, manual labor was the only means to farm. This is still true today in the southwest. Until someone invents a way to collect fruit with a machine, slave labor, or illegal immigrants will have to do the work.

The rich and powerful started segregation to control the masses. They were afraid that the people would rise up and take everything they had. Look at the Boston massacre and other places where people rose up against the wealthy, and burned their homes. The beginning was March 5, 1770, Crispus Attucks was one of the first Americans killed for the American Revolution, and was of African decent. This incident and the November 1, 1765 Stamp Act were some of the first known uprisings against the rich and powerful in this country. Prejudice was very much apart of the Northern culture and not just the south. The rich controlled the education in the country, and made sure only their idea of history was taught. All other history was destroyed, and locked away in history institutions. The minorities in this country were not able to assimilate, because they looked differently. This made it easy to divide and conquer. Look at the overseers on plantations and they were mixed light skin, or low white trash. Also with majority of the population illiterate, and controlling their education made it easier to keep them down. The common thread between people is feeling safe is with your own kind. No matters how hard you try and not be separated. You are still drawn towards your own kind. Example: I heard once there was a group of protesters who went to Washington D.C. to fight for equality. They pitched their tents across from the White House and there were people of all different persuasions and backgrounds. As time went on through the night different people came to the leader to ask if the could move near their friends. In the morning all the groups were segregated. People naturally feel safe with their own kind. I have meet many people who will talk equality, but are married, and all of their friends are one of their own kind.

CHAPTER 4

Segregation as it Exists Today

Government and educational reforms have broken down many of the barriers that I grew up with. The young people of today do not see the stereotypes that were place upon us as children. They date and marry who they want, and do not feel obligated to follow in the footsteps of the past. At the same time there is still an enormous amount of prejudice that still exists in our society today. This is because long-standing laws and institutions have prevailed to coexist with today's society. These institutions are prisons, laws, corrupt government, and religious institutions that are an oxymoron to our society. This is because our government relies on experts to tell them what to do about things. This all started back during WWII when propaganda was becoming an artful science. It started these think tanks where a group of experts would think through different scenarios. When the sixties came there was a sudden transparency that the government did not like called the media? Not only did it allow the world to see what was going on in the war, but also throughout America. President Johnson and Martin Luther King used the media as a catalyst to push equal rights and voting. This caused an immediate divide in the country that caused a firestorm of revolution of equal rights. The problem with this is the media disproportionally divided the nation into two groups. There were conservative white males and everyone else was liberal. This division is still in effect today. It has hampered progress in many endeavors by many different groups. The same as saying all Asians, Black's, Hispanics, Gays, and Women are the same. My first wife was from Thailand and she did not consider herself the same as someone from the Philippines. I also had known people who were Jamaican who did not consider themselves African American. And people I know who are Mexican are not the same as someone from Spain. So why do we lump all these different types of people into categories that do not pertain to them. Because it is convent to do so by people who don't want to see people as individuals. This is what the experts do. They lump people into categories so politicians can make decisions. The politicians place people into areas and make it a political agenda. Look at any city and city planners have cutup the cities by economic graphics. Each city has its main, north, south, east, and west streets. The rich and poor areas will not have very many stores at all. Most stores are in the middle class areas. The rich housing is all gated or demographically displace from the rest of the city. The poor areas will have convenience, liquor and maybe a grocery store. Most big box stores lie on the crust between the poor and middle class. Usually in the older established neighborhoods. This not an inconvenience to the rich, because they can drive to anywhere they need to go. But the poor will have to take buses, trains, or taxis to get there.

The problem with segregation today is more economics and education. People who are economically displaced do not have the same opportunities than someone who is economically secure. There are many programs today that are trying to break down this barrier. They have had some success, but at the cost of lowering standards. Lowering the standards is not helping but hindering the person ability to better themselves. Its like saying we know your stupid, but here you can still do it. We are insulting the individual, and the person who can perform the task.

CHAPTER 5

The Hispanic Endeavor

When I hear that politicians are reaching out to the Hispanic vote. I have to stop and wonder whom are they talking about? My wife now is of Mexican decent, and so is her family. They are all Americans who shop, and do all the things that the rest of America does. The only difference is they have held onto their heritage with language and food. They still go to fast food restaurants to eat tacos, pizza, hamburgers, etc. Now you would ask me if they are Mexican Americans or Americans. I would have to say Americans with a Mexican heritage, and some still with Mexican citizenship. To place another countries name before America would mean you had just came here, and became a citizen. If not, the other countries name has no business being there. This distortion of identity has lead to a lot of problems in the Southwestern United States. It has caused for a type of slavery, and identity crises for the Hispanic population. A person of Hispanic descent and is multi-generation American born and raised. Who can't get a minimum wage job here, unless they say they are illegal. This is because "illegal's will take jobs Americans wont take"; also business will not hire you. Because, they will have to pay you minimum wage, workman's compensation, and take care of you if you get hurt.

A minimum wage worker cost an employer about fifteen dollars an hour. An illegal worker will work for about half of minimum wage, no workmen's compensation, and the Emergency Room will take care of them if they get hurt. Workman's compensation cost an employer about eight dollars more an hour. This disparity between illegal and American born goes way back. If you look at what Caesar Chavez was trying to accomplish, which was to stop illegal immigration. This was because American born Hispanics could not get decent wages or respect. It is better today, but there is still this disparity between them. The government still believes big business. When they say that illegal's are keeping the cost of food products down. Just look at the price of a loft of bread or a gallon of milk that is almost five dollars each. The whole illegal system allows for people to live outside the law, and at the same time protected by the law? Why is the government rewarding people who break the law, and come down so hard on people who up hold the law? The answer is quite simple. The government is slowly eroding our rights and to make more of us dependent upon them. Or is it another completely separate economic system developed for the poor to boost the economies of nations. As in the English gave to China almost all their gold and silver for tea. In order to get a return on their money they started the opium trade. Also Pirate's were used by Spain, Britain, and France to steal from the other without notice. The British were making a fortune out the back door to pirates for goods and services. This went until a tsunami came and destroyed the island.

CHAPTER 6

Control and Power

This controlling the minorities in this nation has been placed upon the heads of the religious leaders in the ghettos. These religious leaders at the time were Christians, and backed the government in helping keep conditions under control. But with the rise of Malcolm-X, a different religion took hold of the black ghettos. It was from a Muslim religion that our government officials did not understand. The same misunderstanding happened during, and after 911. The government appealed to the Black religious leaders who were not like Martin Luther King in trying to untie all people. The new religious leaders saw a divide that the news and television media capitalized on, and so did they. The media divided everyone as old white supremacy and the rest, meaning Blacks, Hispanics, Minorities, Gays, and Women. In turn they placed white guilt upon all white people. Blaming them for all the atrocities, that was placed upon all minorities. This white guilt with the protest of equality in America has given rise to a new socialist class in America.

Go to any university or government agency and you will find this new socialist philosophy at work. In America people love to have a bad guy, and the conservative white male is it. All the worlds' woes are placed upon his shoulders. Also political correctness is also apart of the philosophy. But what is left out of the equation is the fact that it is better here in America, than anywhere else in the world. Which is why so many people are trying anyway they can just to get here. Why, because the poor live better here than most middle class people anywhere else. Really there is no middle class elsewhere, because all other countries are ruled, and not govern by the people. Take for example Mexico: I have been in college classes, and students think Mexico is ruled like the United States. These students were Mexican decent. They did not know that Mexican is not a race, but a group of races making up what is now Mexico. Because a few of hundred years ago the America's was a melting pot of races and nationalities. "(Webster's Ninth New Collegiate Dictionary: (Mexican: …(1600) 1 a: a native or inhabitant of Mexico b: a person of Mexican decent c: *Southwest:* a person of Spanish and Indian decent…)." There is also the French who ruled Mexico and all the slaves that were brought to South America. So when you say Mexican, it is really a mix of races.

This not surprising since the history of our world has been distorted by the very people who believe in the new socialist societies that is dictating to all of us now. They are the elitist and well educated, and are only a handful of scholars who are pushing political correctness. They were also the one's who supported racial bigotry in the past. They were the one's behind making hippies look appealing to America with television sitcoms. They are also the one's who take gangster rap and turns it into Hip-Hop. They allow the minority to degrade themselves and other minorities. While at the same time telling white people not to say certain words. But now in movies they are using the shock and awe of racism to the big screen.

If you lookup Confidentiality Laws of California Laws for Minors you would find it disturbing, because it does not follow with the will of the people, or American idealisms. The statistics for 19 year old un-married mothers show that less than 1% will live, and grow up to be productive citizens. This means not in prison or on some form of social welfare. The government and the college curriculum are also dictated by a group of liberal minded socialist that believe in their agenda. Their agenda is the racial divide that is tearing at the fiber of this country, with this us (minorities) against them (conservative white male) mentality. Martin Luther King had it right when he wanted to break down the racial divide and have racial equality. The path we are on now is making laws not for and by the people, but is being dictated by the elitist. Because of this, is why we are having the mass protest in the streets against the police, and the Judicial System?

CHAPTER 7

The Judicial System

The Judicial System in this country has gotten completely out of control. There were only about 375,000 people in the Judicial System back in 1978. Now there are over ten million in California alone. If you look at the statistics you will see that if ten people committed a crime and went to jail at $33,000 a year. Nine out of ten would be back in prison, but if you rehabilitate same ten criminals at $14,000 a year. Then seven out ten would not go back to jail, and be productive citizens. The reason is the lawyers are pushing legislation to increase the police, prisons, and laws governing the people. They are doing this by advertising pseudo-science and fear to the people. This is why we have more prisons in California than Colleges. The people are now starting to call the Judicial System the "Nanny State". The Judicial System is no longer serving and protecting the average American right of freedom. Instead it is profiling all of us as criminals.

The police Departments motto was to "Serve and Protect" now its "Professional Law Enforcement". Every time there is an attack against the American Government or the Banking institutions our rights are eroded, and become privileges. In the Prison System it is far worst, were the moment you enter you have to join a gang. Human rights violations and prejudice is rampant. There is no real rehabilitation, and prisoners take what they learn back to the streets with them. Most will never come out, and if they do get out. They will find a way to go right back in. Our society has become a work, store, institutional recreation and play. We have developed a society that is starting to closely resemble Northern Europe.

The District Attorneys and lawyers are playing "lets make a deal" when a common person is arrested. They can do this because they have unlimited resources at hand. Also the judges will side with the lawyers and police, before they side with a common person. A Non-Common Person: is someone who is in Law Enforcement, Government or

Diplomatic Immunity, Religious Leader, and Famous or Rich. "Let's make a Deal" is a term I use to describe a District Attorney who will offer someone a deal. Say a person is wrongfully arrested for a crime they did not commit. But there is enough circumstantial evidence to convict them, which is the policemen's word against yours. The District Attorney offers you eight months in prison and some probation time for a confession. Which should have you out in about eight weeks with good behavior, or the maximum sentence of ten to thirty years when convicted. An honest person would never agree to this and gets the maximum sentence. Where the criminal who always has ether something to give to the police or knows better, and takes the deal. This is why the criminals seem to do little jail time, and they are back on the streets in no time. With this revolving door for the criminals the lawyers can scare the good citizen into passing legislation requiring more police and prisons. Also the prisons have a huge racial divide between races because of the need for survival. The liberal socialist, have taken away the prison guards control. The guards are only there to keep the prisoners in and not to control, and protect the inmates.

The police departments are racial profiling minorities. This is because in the minority community where the population is over 60% in the Judicial System. This means the police see all of them as criminals. Which means they have the right to pull you over, and throw you against a police car anytime they see you. This is from the time you are old enough to eat at the table, until you're old and grey. When you have seen all of your relative's and friend's, both men and women treated in this manner being beaten and killed. It does something to you. With most of the policemen who are white and even the minorities' policemen think poorly of there own kind. This racial divide has caused a lot of racial haltered, and a calloused attitude. If you think this is an unjust description of the police. Then I would suggest that you go to the poor minority part of town after hours. Then contest your rights to the policemen who pull you over. Then go to a middle class neighborhood and see if you get pulled over. You will if you're a minority wearing a hoodie or more than two of you in the car. Mainly see the difference the way police treat you, especially if you are white. Also if you are black and grew up in the middle class, and go to a black neighborhood, and see how differently you are treated. Do the same if you are white, it will be an education in humility. This difference is where most white people will have a hard time understanding. The difference between someone who is black, and someone who was raised ghetto. They think the difference is only the color of your skin. They don't understand that you were raised with a complete different set of scruples and morals. They do not understand the anger in your heart towards them, and the world that you live in. The people who were raised in middle class America are raised differently. Where you raise your hand in class, and say yes sir, and yes mam. Taught to respect your elders, and people in authority. They grow up in a structured environment with love, respect, and all needs meet. A person from the ghetto is raised to hate school, people of authority, and raised in a completely unstructured environment. There is no love in their lives, and have to fend for themselves for their basic needs. The gap between the two groups is so wide that one is a reverse culture to the other. This disparity between the two groups has caused a ripple effect throughout the country.

Chapter 8

Urban Sprawl

This countrywide disparity is what the Ghetto Effect is. It use to be contained in the ghettos, but now it has spread throughout the country. This is because the social elitist has developed urban sprawl to get rid of the government housing. Government housing was at one time made to bring the poor blacks from the south to the north in promise of jobs. The jobs the elitist had in mind was to clean the cities, and do sanitation, gardening, and to be a nanny for rich people's children. Instead it became a cesspool of multigenerational crime and gangs. When equal rights came into play and a decline in factories in the cities. All the whites moved out and the blacks moved in. The areas around the downtown districts fell into chaos. If you look at Detroit it looks like a nuclear bomb went off in the middle of what use to be the most beautiful neighborhood in America. Now this ghetto mentality has become apart of every city in America. This spread is due to the section 8 project, which is to give every person a home. This is the solution to the government-housing problem. By having urban sprawl to separate the masses it will divide and conquer the poor. They do this by having housing developers make low cost housing. Then have people who can't afford a house, buy into one. They are usually in the house long enough to pay off the initial building cost. Then they file bankruptcies or default on the loan. Finally the government can come in and take it over from the bank. This how the Government makes section 8 housing. So now you have the government or the owner of a house who chooses to have their house up for section 8 maintaining the property. Also you have people who can't afford a home nor maintain it, living in a home nicer than the homes a working class person can afford. This section 8 housing also includes illegal aliens.

CHAPTER 9

Two Flawed Economies

What we end up with is two different types of economies living inside a democracy that is flawed. People are finally starting to catch on that criminals have more and better rights than the honest citizen. Example: There are now elderly people who are committing crimes to get surgeries, medicines, medical procedures, and dental work done. Now a person who goes to jail for drugs and criminal activity gets Social Security SSI. Which is more than my wife makes being retired with Social Security. They are given the pay they earn while being incarcerated. Also the criminals are given free health, and dental care. They are given a social worker who helps them get a job, and if unskilled paid to go to school. The criminal is also setup with a hotel room until they can find him or she a place to live. Myself on the other hand who is retired from the Military Service received $480 a month in retirement pay. I pay $460 a year for medical, which no doctor in my area now will take, because it's a HMO. My dental service was $64 a month. My employer has the same dental company, for the same price, and better coverage. I had received $10 a year raises until 2008, which stopped. When I got out of the service I had no workman's compensation. No unemployment compensation, because I quit my job. Only what the government owed me for unpaid leave. An I.D. card (expiration date: Indefinite) to use government services at bases worldwide. My education benefit was the V.E.A.P. Program where every dollar I put in the government put in $2 up to $100 a month, a total of $10,000 dollars. I had ten years to use it or loose it. I never used it.

The two economies that I speak of is one is the Legal System and the other is the Illegal System. The legal System is where you pay your taxes. Have a driver's license, and work for a living. These people live in a very small box that allows them to shop, work, and play at institutions. They are held accountable for all of their actions. They pay the lion's share of the taxes. This is because taxes are paid to an "earned income". People who are rich have portfolios and are not required to pay taxes, and do not have an earned income. The rich have property in many states but only claim the state that does not require state tax. So they don't pay state or federal income taxes. The rich also promote programs for the poor to which the middle class pays for.

The illegal system on the other hand allows large sums of money to float around without control. One of the known things in the world is that there is always going to be 10% of the population that is poor and 10% rich. The rest of us make up the rest. There is and have always been a silent set of society that prays on the rest. The governments of the world have figured out a way to exploit it. In order to offset its financiers with China for tea. The British Government started the Opium Trade. The made up Cold War was to get rid of all the killers from WWII and Korea. It started a world wide illegal system that is still in play today. Once you are apart of the system you will never get out. This silent but ever useful part of society is beginning to clash with the legal society. To a point that its on the verge of crashing. Legalizing pot, and citizens wanting reforms in the judicial system is causing waves.

CHAPTER 10

Veterans and a Failed School System

All veterans are lumped into the same category and are made to look pathetic, homeless, and dangerous. This is the same image that is pushed to show the poor. The pathetic part is that the common person can no longer own his or her own business. If you go to any convenience store across America you will see people from other countries running them. This is because the government offsets their startup cost and they get huge tax breaks. This is because this is how they made a living from where they are from. Also through taxation and legislation pushed through by big business and special interest groups. The homeless part is also not true of most veterans, but a very real reality for the common person. This in part the government and the school system are still working on the same premise. That high school is to prepare young minds for college. This is a fallacy of misconception, because colleges are no longer preparing students for the job market. Instead they are taking the money and giving out subjugated scholarships.

The city mangers, and the ruling class of the day designed high schools. This means if you live in a farming area you will have farming program. If you live in a city that has a lot of theaters, then theatrics will be the prime courses in the school. If the school is in upper middle class, then business classes will prevail. If the school is in the poor areas then you get the rejected teachers and curriculum on the elementary level. This is why most adults go to adult skill orientated, two year schools. They also join the military to get the skills and college needed to get a good job. So they usually go back to school when they get out. In order to get what they wanted by the military in the first place. When I got out twenty years ago the military was trying to give credit to personnel for the skills acquired in the military to translate to civilian life. Which means a Electronic Technician, Electrician, or a Mechanic, can get a job as what he was trained to do in the military as a civilian.

This school philosophy to prepare our children for college is a fallacy. College was never made for the poor, but for the upper classes. It was to prepare their children to go into the business world to take over global empires. This is why the military and our social systems seem similar. You have the officers, commission officer, non-commission officers, and enlisted. The status quos of our society dictates to the rest of us the way we are to behave. This status quos of our society are the same ones who are pushing all of the liberal bias down our throats. Which is why no one is noticing the Ghetto Effect that is going on in today's society. The Ghetto Effect is very subtle and yet very much in everyone's face.

CHAPTER 11

Urban Traumatic Stress Syndrome (UTSS)

Everyone has heard of Post Traumatic Stress Disorder (PTSD). It took years for the government to recognize it as real problem. Urban Traumatic Stress Syndrome (UTSS) is just as much of a disorder that has yet to be diagnosed. The problem with diagnosing this syndrome is the symptoms. The people who live in these areas are a very diverse group of people. You have people with mental heath issues that are both genetic and chemically induced. There is a large group of homeless people who are both economically disenfranchised and mentally incapable of holding a job. There are multigenerational career criminals and criminal offenders, who cannot live anywhere else. There is rampant illegal drug and alcohol use, with prescription drug abuse. There are also children having children, and women whose men are incarcerated. These women are not bad people who enjoy having children by so many men, but the situation they are in makes it so.

The police are not all bad, but like the school system. The bad one's are taken out of the suburbs, and placed in the urban school districts. The police and the judges have to work together in order to maintain the law that is given to them by the people. Lawyers persuade the people, and the government. Who are out to make money, and a career for themselves? They use their power and money to manipulate the media. Then pursued the people that what they are doing is for the greater good of society. The experts justify their endeavors by showing the statistics that prove what they are doing is right.

If a solider can be traumatize by seeing his buddy killed. Then how much more traumatized are these people living in these urban jungles traumatized? If everyday you left your house. A policeman threw you to the ground or placed you against a wall, or police car and searched you. How long would you stand for it, before you would not want to cooperate any longer? If everyone you know including mother, father, sister, brother, aunts, and uncles were beaten, killed, falsely accused, and placed in a cage like an animal. How long would it take before you would rebel against such an aggressor? Would it take days, weeks, years, decades, or generations before you did something? It's even harder when you don't have the knowledge, skills or the ability to do so. There are so many organizations that have so many programs to help the individual problem, but not to address the root cause of the problem.

CHAPTER 12

The Solution

The answer is very simple we need to treat each other with love and respect. These are missing from our culture today. A famous black comedian came under attack for speaking his mind. When he talked about the youth in the entertainment industry. He called them on acting and behaving in a manner unbecoming to their stature. The different group's, who were racially biased, attacked him. He threw it back in their face, and got them to see the relativity of their bias. As of lately the only form of honest reporting is through comedy. It's as if a late night talk show can get away with telling the truth, but honest reporting is castigated. Also the reporting needs to be positive journalism. This done through Social journalism that takes a more open-minded approach to journalism.

The reality is that the urban ghetto needs to be dismantled and the people need to be healed. This heeling is done, by empowering the people to be in control of their neighborhoods. The people who are in need of mental health services need to be removed, and taken care of. Mental institutions need to be rebuilt. The career criminal should not be placed back into decent society, until they can be properly rehabilitated. The police need to have manors training. Everyone that I meet in customer service have the worst attitudes. This is because they are dealing with situations that they are not trained to handle. With the proper instruction they can learn restraint. Having the religious organizations and watchdog groups help in the policing of the people, and the police. Body cameras and dash cameras, are also a good thing to have implemented.

The federal government could have watchdog group's setup to monitor the mental health of the neighborhoods. They could go door to door and ask questions. Example: How many times have you been stopped by the police? Did you do anything to warrant the stop? Have you ever been assaulted by the police? Was the assault justified? Do you have a means of supporting yourself? If not, then what are your plans for in the future? Is there anything the city or the government can do to assist you? Have you thought of starting up your own business? What can the city or government do to assist you? Are you registered to vote? Have you been to a town hall meeting, and given your voice to help your community?

Teen pregnancies are not controlled or stopped by giving out contraceptives and condoms. By giving young people options will deter teen pregnancies. When young people see a future, they usually self inflict restraint. A young person, who is sexually molested, or sexually active at a young age, will usually teach what they learn to others their age. Just as people who have low intelligent levels will persuade others with less intelligent to do crimes, so they wont get caught.

In order to break the cycle of abuse and bulling the attitudes have to be addressed. The only thing I know that is strong enough is love, patients, and respect. (1 Corinthians 13:4-8, New International Version) "4 Love is patient, love is kind. It does not envy, it does not boast, it is not proud. 5 It is not rude, it is not self-seeking, it is not easily angered, it keeps no record of wrongs. 6 Love does not delight in evil but rejoices with the truth. 7 It always protects, always trusts, always hopes, always preserves. 8 Love never fails."

This religious text that I quote is because the truth is self-evident. That all who read its contents knew that the truth is for all people. This disparity between what people feel and what people know never helps no one, but only blinds the truth. When the truth is revealed there is no argument to be made. We can continue along the same path of self-destruction. Or we can start to try and heal and comfort a people who need our help. These are people who can't help themselves.

CHAPTER 13

My Beginnings

My beginnings start in Hapeville a suburb of Atlanta Georgia. My father was a WWII Vet, 101st Company "E". My mother was a candy store clerk on Chicago's South Side when they meet. He was going to college to become a dentist, then change, and became an optometrist. He passed away right after my fifth birthday and my mother became a full-blown schizophrenic. So my two older sisters (Marguerite and Evelyn) and me lived with relatives for a year, while our mother was institutionalized. We lived on our grandparent's farm (father side) for the summer in Indiana. Then were forcible taken by the sheriffs to live with our mothers oldest sister in Maryland. Her husband was an Officer in the Navy and worked at the Pentagon. They were willed to take care of us. They thought our grandparents were less than suitable caregivers of us. Especially after they came to visited us. They saw me running around in just short pants with no shirt or shoes. We lived in their basement all in one bed. I was their daughter's whipping boy, when she did something wrong.

When our mother finally got out of the institution. We all went to live with her mother in her apartment in South Shore on Chicago's South Side, 77th and Colfax Ave. My mother's brother lived with his mother, who was never married, and never had a girl friend. He smelled, and would punish me almost everyday for running home, or tearing my pants by falling. He would do so by making me stand in the corner. We lived in an apartment building that had a bay window that jetted out. So he had a clear view of the street that I came down. My mother, two sisters and me all shared the same bed. Mom's mother and father came from Germany and she would make German food with a lot of black pepper, which I didn't care for. I was never allowed to go outside and play, so I didn't have any friends, except one. He was really nice Jewish boy who taught me how to play chess. I played with his grandfather and won. He asked me how I got so smart? I told him my grandmother says that because I am German, and that I am smarter than everyone else. So I was never allowed to play with him again. I did have an imaginary bear named Max that was huge, and would talk to me at the window.

When we first got to Chicago I thought my back was going to break from the cold. I always wore dress shoes until I was a teenager. I never had any foul weather clothing other than two pairs of socks or pants. After a year of living with relatives we finally got our own place two apartments down from grandmas. I was finally able to go out and play, and make friends. My sisters starting to notice boys, and my second oldest sister Evelyn fell in love with her future husband. Who she is still married to today. It was at this time in history that not only did my world changed, but also the nations. For this was around 1969 to 1970 and I got to witness first hand the violent upheaval of Chicago first hand.

One time, while living in our new apartment. There was a black man who lived below us. His wife came home and caught him with a white woman. They were yelling and screaming. He chased her across the street and shot her with a shotgun. Then the police arrived and shot him. Once my sisters convinced my mother to have a party and all these older kids came, and they played spin the bottle, and post office. I kissed my first girl then who was thirteen and I was 10. I later became good friends with these two girls who lived in a house on the corner of 78th and Colfax. One day a black teenage boy was trying things with the two girls. I jumped in to stand up for them. He beat me down and stomped on my face. I was very naive at the time. My school started letting more black children in, because my neighborhood was fairly liberal minded. I had this black boy in my class who would ask me for money. I said yes because I had got a couple of dollars for my birthday. He wanted me to bring him it. I said I couldn't because it was my birthday money. So he said you could bring me a quarter, so I said ok. Then he expected me to bring him another quarter the next day, and the day after. I finally stood up to him, and he punched in the throat. I am still to this day able to push my throat out like a frog today because of it.

CHAPTER 14

My Golden Years of Equal Rights

We finally moved because our neighborhood was becoming more violent. Instead of us moving away we moved deeper into the neighborhood, to 73rd and Coles Ave. The summer of 5th grade most white people moved away from our lovely neighborhood, and Rainbow Park became a battlefield. We moved here because my sister was in love with her future husband. We got an apartment above an elderly couples house. The dead-end street 73rd and Exchange Ave. became my hangout, until I joined the Submarine Service at 18.

During this teenage time I was no longer allowed to hang out with my sisters, when I turned 13. I was told to hang out with my sister's boyfriend Ricky's younger brother Eugene, whom I had known since living on Colfax Avenue.

When we meet I was taught not to fight, and turn the other cheek. Eugene and his two older brothers were streetwise, and did not turn the other cheek. I meet my second best friend Paul by Eugene fighting him, because I wouldn't. Paul wanted to beat me up because I broke his ruler. This was because I was watching some guy's cutup trees in front of my apartment on Colfax. One of them was breaking limbs with his bear hands. I had asked him where he learned this, and he said the World War II. I told him about my father, and so he showed me how to do it. I had practiced, and broke a pencil in classroom. The kid next to me asked if I could break a ruler. So I said yes, and broke mine. Then he inquired if I could break two rulers, and I said sure easily. So he took his and Paul's ruler. Who was sitting behind me and I broke them, before Paul could protest. So Paul saw me after school as the school code goes, and the rest is history.

Needless to say before I turned thirteen. Paul and me use to hang out together, and play Army. But when I started to hang out with what we eventually called ourselves the dead-end gang. "We were in no way a real gang." We were just a bunch of kids who hung around together. We went swimming at the beach, played street football, basketball, and eventually alcohol. Most of the kids were two or more years older, and taught me a lot of bad things like drinking and smoking. The one thing they could not do was to change the scruples that my parents and relatives had instilled into me before. These Christian and American based idealisms grounded my sisters and me from doing a lot of bad things other people we knew did. They were growing up in the American middle class. An example was when we were living with our aunt and uncle in Maryland and we went to a Pentagon dinner function. A few days before someone wrote in big letters F__ Y__. In red paint on the street near our house. I got to meet President Johnson and he ask me if there was any question, that he could answer that no one else could. Well after my father died I became violently obsessed when people would not tell me something I wanted to know. This is because they would not talk about my father if I were in the room. So they would make me leave and I got a compulsion disorder from it. So the president said: "that it was bad words and we needed to clean up our streets" and went away.

I had become a wino at thirteen and started smoking cigarettes. My grade school went from a predominately white, to predominately black school after the summer of fifth grade. Almost all the white people left all at once one summer. Then violence escalated. My entire circle of friends was multiracial. I would stand up for black friends at school, who were picked on by other black kids. In 5th grade Martin Luther King was killed and hundreds' of black kids were going around beating any white kids they could find. We were just getting out of school. When my future brother in-laws sister was attacked by a mob. Her younger sister jumped in, but could not fight them all. Their use to be gangs of kids 60 strong who would just run around the streets.

Our education level at school went from an 8th grade reading level to a kindergarten level in 6th grade. We had kids in our class right out of reform school who were 16 and 17 years old. They would rob us boys and molest the girls. By the time we went into 7th grade. We had girls coming up pregnant, which was unheard of at the time. It had become a reverse culture than what I was use to. What was good was then bad, and what was bad was then good. There were girls in my class that were multi-generation prostitutes. Most of the kids I was in class with did not have both parents, and did not know their fathers. There were prostitutes on the corner of South Shore drive near the hotel we use to go swimming at on the corner of 75th street. All alone 75th street there was bars with pimp cars (Cadillac's with white fur, and big chrome and gold grills.). Most families all lived in one apartment from grandparents on down. All classes of people were thrown together to live. Majority of the population had criminal records. Drugs, alcohol and crime ran rampant. I knew boys who would snatch purses; rob houses, and anything they could. It was not like white America where you had upper, middle, and lower class areas. Here the well to do, policemen, professor, and criminal all were forced to live together. The neighborhoods in Chicago were segregated in Polish, Greek, Italian, Jewish, Mexican, Puerto Rican, Black, and different Asian cultures. These areas were separated by demographics like a railroad track or a large road. Everyone stayed in their neighborhood or would get hurt venturing into another, without business or reason.

Also in 7th grade on Dr. Martin Luther King birthday in 1973 at 8:45 am every kid in the school (Myra Bradwell 7736 S. Burham Ave.) put their head on their desk. As the last 3 white boys in my school was executed on the catwalk behind the vice principles office. The first was shot in the head and the other two ran, and was gunned down. They had tried to kill me numerous times, but I was able to survive. Once I helped a boy who I didn't know. I kept seeing him being beat up by this other black boy. I beat up the other boy and later his brother and his cousin. The boy befriended me by asking me to walk him home. When we got to the corner of 71st. Yates Ave. he said he was sorry, and he was made to do it. Then some men from across the tracks started shooting at me with a small caliber pistol until it was empty, and then I ran home. Another time I was going to school. This older boy came out from behind a building with a sawed off hunting rifle. He had a brown paper bag over it, and was aiming it at me. Then I saw a police car, so I threw my hands in the air, and said don't shoot. He got nerviest and the bag fell off. The police jumped out of their car, and demand he drop the rifle. He turned toward them, and they shot him, while I ran to school. Also in grade school I got into a fight with all the black kids around me for singing the National Anthem {a teacher and me was the only one's singing}. Then I got into another fight right after, for not singing the Black Nation Anthem. Another time, 20-30 black kids attacked me; they wanted to hurt me real bad. I had managed to get to the landing to the back door of the school. I held the high ground beating off all who came up the stairs. The teacher would not open the door and let me in. I had to jump down and walk out, while fighting to the front of the school. My last day in Myra Bradwell

Elementary School was graduation day. My mother and sisters came to see me graduate. I had gotten into two fights down stairs in the basement before the ceremony, and two more during the ceremony. This is because all the leading black leaders of Chicago's South Side were in the 71st street Baptist church. They were calling my mother the white devil, and all kinds of stuff I injected upon. Which is why I was fighting for my mothers honor.

There are many wondrous stories I could tell you about Chicago and police brutality. I have seen them beat my friends and arrest people I know for unwanted crimes. My friends in the suburbs would take their fathers car and get caught and it's called joy ridding. Kids in my neighborhood it was called grand thief auto. I was at Marquette Park on the west side, and Calumet Park on the east side, during the equal rights demonstrations. My High School Bowen in South Chicago, 87th st, and in a predominately Hispanic community. We would have riots once a month between the Black and Mexican kids. The school was half and half, with 10% Puerto Rican which no one messed with. Then there were about 10 white trash kids, and I was one of them. The school was split between two neighborhoods. One neighborhood use to be white, but the whites all left, and the blacks move in. The Hispanic group still hated the whites. Of the two major groups, one would rob the other, or mess with the others women, and a riot would be on. There was a police station a block away, but it was too much for them, so they would call in the National Guard. The school was five stories tall with a three-story building attached, and a park across the street.

This is about enough history about me growing up in Chicago. Many of the people I grew up with had very little choices. The choice was School, Prison, or the Military. I would say 1 percent of one percent went to college. Most went to prison or the military. I had seen quite a few guys come back from Vietnam and none were right in the head after. The one's that didn't commit suicide, were forced to join gangs that were ever increasingly violent. I delivered newspapers from age 12 to 16. Then I started to go the west side and deliver groceries for sister Evelyn's future mother in-law. I did that until eighteen and got my drivers license and started driving cars for the Chicago Auto Action.

CHAPTER 15

The Military Solution

I joined the Submarine Service at 18 two months before my ninetieth birthday. I joined the Navy in the Sub-farer program as an E-1. I struck the Interior Communications Division, meaning; I worked towards the rating by qualifying the watch station onboard the submarine. I started out Mess Cranking; which is working for the Cooks. Cleaning dishes and floors by hand, and preparing meals by peeling potatoes and etc. After a year I got qualified in submarines, and was driving my Submarine as a Helmsman/Planesman/Lookout. In the summer of 1980 during a Trident Missile up-grade to our sub in Coco Beach Florida. I applied to Basic Electricity/ Electronics School in Orlando Florida as an E-3 (which is a low ranking enlisted person). Orlando Florida was only one of two female Boot Camps in the Navy, and a Training School Command. I was the first Interior Communications Electrician (I.C.men) in the Navy to complete Modules 1 through 25. Before I.C.men only went to Module 14. If I wanted to continue to module 35 I would have had to reenlist for another two years, and become an electronics technician. I liked what (I.C.men) did, and went back to my sub in Charleston South Carolina were we were Home Ported. The old Fleet Ballistic Missile Submarine's had two crews. One crew would be out on a 90-day patrol, while the other was at its homeport going to school and training.

I was stationed onboard three Fleet Ballistic Nuclear Submarines, three Los Angeles Class Fast Attack Nuclear Submarines. I have a certificate in Human Services: Mental Heath/Substance Abuse, A.S. Degree in Social Science (Phi Theta Kappa), and a B.S. Degree in Workforce Curriculum and Development. Went up to the rank of E-6. After passing the E-7 exam. The Capitan of my 4th boat, my first Fast Attack submarine busted me on made up charges. I had just lost my first wife to Liver Cancer after our 3rd anniversary. When I first joined you couldn't get out of you tried. Then the 90's came, and they changed the rules to where the Capitan's was given the power of Captain's Mast. I volunteered for the Navy's CAC program, which is for drug and alcohol abuse. I didn't do drugs, but I had problems and needed help so I volunteered to get help. I found out years later after I got out that I could not take Statin Drugs for my Cholesterol. The Statin Drugs caused me to not to be able to control my temper. I did have an alcohol incident in the past. Like the time I accidently walked through a radiation boundary the first day at the shipyard on my third sub after drinking. It was 4 o'clock in the morning, and had a string with a small sign on it in the middle of the pier. The width of the pier was like a 4-lane highway. I was sent to alcohol counseling, but that was all. I had attended twenty-five technical and leadership schools. Took one Fleet Ballistic Nuclear Submarine out of Portsmouth Naval Ship Yard and the 1st one in 14 years early. Also a Los Angeles Class Fast Attack Nuclear Submarine out of Mare Island shipyard, 1st in 7 years early. The 1st Interior Communication Electrician to complete Basic Electricity and Electronics School MODS 1 – 25. Naval Instructor and Course Curriculum Model

Manager S.N.A.P.II (Shipboard Non-Tactical Automated Data Processing System). I was one of the, 1st Shipboard Gauge Calibration Petty Officers, and numerous more accolades to my name. I retired early because of a new program they came up with to help get people out of the service. I continued on with my education until now. I am a Hospital Engineer and have published 5 books: Ten Bears to Destiny, Death to Freedom Part I and II, P-IATE KIDS, Pirate Cadet Kids. Married to my wonderful wife Josie. We have 3 children who are all married and 11 grandchildren.

I write this book with a heavy heart. This book is as much about healing myself, as it is about healing a nation. I hope all of you with thin skin's, use this book as a catalyst to strike up the conversation. To use this to correct the wrongs of the past, and not to just degrade the writer. There are lives being torn apart by this insensitive attack, on anyone who stands up for human rights. Please look for the solution, and not the problem. For the time for immature finger pointing is over, and a mature conversation is needed.

References

1.) Philippines Copyright 1991 by Merriam-Webster Inc. Webster's Ninth New Collegiate Dictionary.

2.) Copyright 1970 by Thomas Nelson Inc. Printed Edition in 1996 United States of America. The Holy Bible Old and New Testaments in the King James Version.

3.) United States of America Copyright 1995 by the Zondervan Corporation. The NIV Large Print Study Bible, 10th Anniversary Edition.